Chickens!

Illustrated Chicken Breeds
A to Z

Written and Illustrated by Sarah Rosedahl

*For Jennie
Enjoy!*

Sarah Rosedahl

ISBN-13: 978-0615810799 (Tolba Farm Press)
ISBN-10: 0615810799

Dedication

For Leisa, my family, and friends

who have always supported

my adventures.

Ameraucana

Ameraucanas lay blue eggs and are said to be descendants of the "Quetro" chicken of South America.

✳

Brahma

Brahma chickens originated in China and were known as "Shanghai" birds.

＊

Cochin

Cochins originated in China and were once also known as Shanghai birds. Cochins were adored by Queen Victoria in the mid-1800s.

✳

Derbyshire Redcap

The Derbyshire

Redcap

originated in

England

and derives its

name from its

unusually large

rose-type comb.

✳

Easter Egger

An Easter Egger

is not actually

a breed but

any chicken

that possesses

the "blue egg"

gene.

✳

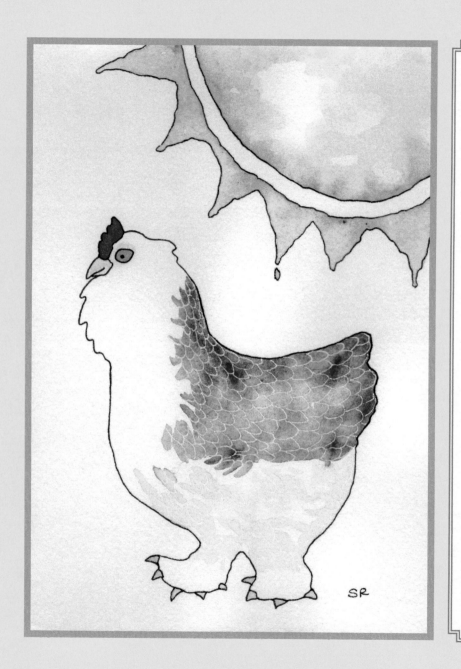

Faverolles

Faverolles is

a French breed,

has a beard,

muffs, five toes

on each foot

and feathered

legs.

*

Gournay

The Gournay is an ancient breed originating from the Normandy region of France.

*

Hamburg

Hamburg chickens originated in Holland. They are flighty birds that prefer to roost in trees and bushes.

＊

Iowa Blue

The Iowa Blue

is a rare breed

that originated

near Decorah,

Iowa. The Iowa

Blue lays

brown eggs.

＊

Jersey Giant

Jersey Giants
are the largest
purebred chicken.
Mature roosters
weigh 12 to 15
pounds.

✳

Kosovo
Long Crowing Rooster

This rooster's

crow averages

20 to 40

seconds.

✻

Leghorn

Leghorns were originally imported to America from Italy and were called "Italians."

＊

Marans

Marans chickens originated in France and are known as "chocolate eggers."

✳

New Hampshire Red

The New
Hampshire Red
was derived
from the Rhode
Island Red and
lays large
brown eggs.

*

Orpington

Orpingtons are big, fluffy birds that were originally bred by William Cook of Orpington, County of Kent, England.

✳

Polish

The Polish chicken
is known for its
crest of feathers.
The breed's name
is said to have
been derived
from the caps
worn by Polish
soldiers.

＊

Quechua

Quechua are

high altitude

chickens of

Northwestern

South America.

✳

Rosecomb

The Rosecomb

is known for

its distinctive

comb. It is one

of the oldest

pure bantam

breeds.

*

Silkie

Silkies have

distinctive

physical

characteristics

including silky

plumage, dark

skin and five

toes on each

foot.

*

Turken
Transylvanian Naked Neck

Turkens don't

have any feathers

on their necks.

They are

rumored to be

part turkey,

but are in fact

chickens.

*

Utrerana

Utrerana is

an old breed that

originated in

Southern Spain

and is now

endangered.

*

Vorwerk

The Vorwerk
originated in
Germany and is
unrelated to
the vacuum
cleaner of the
same name!

*

Wyandotte

Wyandottes originated in the United States in the 1870s. The Wyandotte appears in eight different colors.

*

23

i X worth

The iXworth is

a rare breed that

originated in

Suffolk England.

iXworth hens

typically lay

over 240 eggs

per year.

＊

Yokohama

The Yokohama originated from Japanese breeds. Under ideal conditions the rooster's tail feathers can grow up to three feet per year.

✳

Zilarra

The Zilarra is

a white and black

variety of a

Spanish breed

known as a

"Basque chicken."

*

Made in the USA
Columbia, SC
05 May 2017

Elmo Loves You!

Elmo Loves You!

A Poem by ELMO

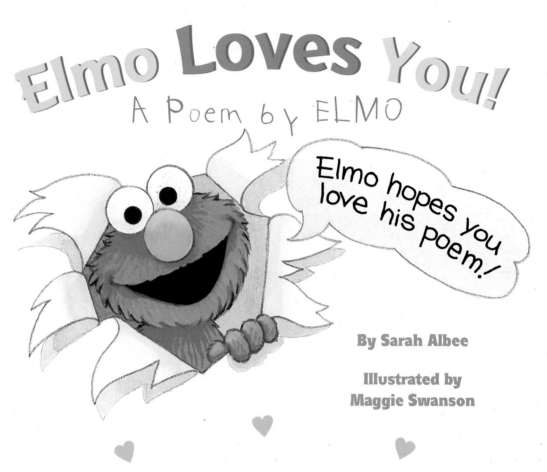

Elmo hopes you love his poem!

By Sarah Albee

Illustrated by Maggie Swanson

Dalmatian Press, LLC, 2005. All rights reserved.
Published by Dalmatian Press, LLC, 2005. The DALMATIAN PRESS name and logo are trademarks of Dalmatian Press, LLC, Franklin, Tennessee 37067. No part of this book may be reproduced or copied in any form without written permission from the copyright owner.

Printed in the U.S.A.
ISBN: 1-40371-694-3 (X) 1-40372-106-8 (M)

07 08 LBM 10 9 8 7 6
14732 Sesame Street 8x8 Storybook: Elmo Loves You!

Everyone loves something.
Babies love noise.
Birds love singing.

Kids love toys.

Bert loves pigeons,
and pigeons love to coo.
Can you guess who Elmo loves?
Elmo loves *you!*

Piggies love to roll in mud.

Penguins love the snow.

Farmers love to wake up early.
Roosters love to crow.

Zoe loves the library. Grover loves it, too.
Elmo whispers quietly, "Elmo loves *you!*"

The Count loves counting things.

How does Elmo love you? Let me count the ways!

Ernie loves to drum.

Monsters love to
exercise.

Everyone loves something.
Elmo told you this was true.
And now you know who Elmo loves:
Elmo loves *you!*

Before Elmo ends his poem,
Elmo wants to ask you this:
Will you be Elmo's valentine?
Can Elmo have a kiss?

What are some things that you love?